MOTHER POEM

EDWARD KAMAU BRATHWAITE

Mother Poem

Oxford   New York

OXFORD UNIVERSITY PRESS

Oxford University Press, Walton Street, Oxford OX2 6DP

Oxford New York Toronto
Delhi Bombay Calcutta Madras Karachi
Petaling Jaya Singapore Hong Kong Tokyo
Nairobi Dar es Salaam Cape Town
Melbourne Auckland

and associated companies in
Beirut Berlin Ibadan Nicosia

First published 1977
Reprinted 1979, 1982, 1988

British Library Cataloguing in Publication Data

Brathwaite, Edward
Mother poem.
I. Title
821   PR9230.9.B/   77–30091
ISBN 0–19–211859–5

Printed in Great Britain by
J. W. Arrowsmith Ltd, Bristol

for
Odale
Bebe
and the memory of
Amy Clementina Skeete
1900–1973

ACKNOWLEDGEMENTS

Because of the nature and structure of this poem, I have offered very little for pre-publication; the exceptions being 'Cherries' in *Giant talk: an anthology of Third World writings*, edited by Quincy Troupe & Rainer Schulte (New York, 1975); 'Dais' and 'Nights' as *Days & Nights*, a limited edition with Barry Higman's Caldwell Press (Mona, 1975); and 'Angel/Engine' with *Alcheringa* (vol. 2, no. 1, 1976).

I should also like to thank the John Guggenheim Memorial Foundation whose generous Fellowship allowed me time to write and work on this poem during 1972/73.

CONTENTS

PREFACE

This poem is about porous limestone: my mother, Barbados: most English of West Indian islands, but at the same time nearest, as the slaves fly, to Africa. Hence the protestant pentecostalism of its language, interleaved with Catholic bells and kumina. The poem is also about slavery (which brought us here) and its effect upon the manscape. So we find my mother having to define her home as plot of ground—the little she can win and own—and the precious seedling children planted for the future. But that plot and plan is limited and constantly threatened or destroyed by the plantation and the fact that the males of her life have become creatures, often agents, of the owner-merchant. Hence the water-lessness of 'Rock Seed', the first nine statements of the sequence.

Parts II and III, 'Nightwash' and 'Tuk', show the effect of pressure on the woman. With her men crippled, destroyed, frightened, or sick (the result of their in-bondage), she has to venture out into the 'mercantile shame/rock', helping to 'make enns meet'. She is forced into a series of expedients, ending in prostitution, love-loss, and abortion; though it is at this very moment of *extremis* that she discovers her underground resources (her *nam*), expressed in the deadly game-conflicts of 'Nametracks', 'Dais' and 'Nights'; so that in Part IV, 'Koumfort', as the poem nears its end, the mother is beginning . . .

we're the first potential parents who can contain the ancestral house . . .

Wilson Harris, *The Whole Armour*

I

ROCK SEED

Alpha

The ancient watercourses of my island
echo of river, trickle, worn stone,
the sunken voice of glitter inching its pattern to the sea,
memory of foam, fossil, erased beaches high above the eaten
    boulders of st philip

my mother is a pool

once there was trail glass, tinkle of stream into gullies
the harbour river navigable for miles
josé, the water of the portuguese
almost ready for rafting

my mother sits above these on her mountain

curl, leaf of dreamer
drift plantations away
i remember ancient watercourses
dead streams, carved footsteps

and my mother rains upon the island with her loud voices

with her grey hairs
with her green love

2

open the door now
and watch from the verandah
the grey street where my father works

he has gone out among bicycle bells
gunfire of donkey carts
fishsellers' cries

ayeeeee . . . . . haaaay

he knocks on the door of the warehouse
and the thin skinned merchant lets him in
marker of bags, maker of chalk dust, white

man of sugar

and my father swims through the noise
through the blankets of jute on his lungs

and he is caesar again at the hellespont

school book, school bag of memory,
climbing the clattering stairs to disaster or prize

he has gone out to the world columbus found
to the world raleigh raided
to the plantation ground

while my mother sits and calls on jesus name

she waits for his return
with her gold rings of love
with the miner's trove that binds her to his world

she waits with her back
slowly curving to mountain
from the deeps of her poor soul

3

when the roll is called up yonder
when the roll is called up yonder
when the roll is called up yonder
when the roll is called up yonder i'll be there

Twine

My husband
if you cud see he
fragile, fraid o' e own shadow
he does let de man boss e 'bout in de job
like e got a dog in de corner

i know when i did first meet e
he did strong
smellin strong o carbolic lotion
an de dirty jokes he did tell de taffeta women on de excursion
    train out to t'ickets

i know when i did first meet e
he did look like e cudda wrench de wrongs
off de sweet drink bottles wid e teef
an tek what he want *so*, an drink it

an he did wear dem two-tone shoes
an a wesscoat, an dat tie-pin, man,
you cud *wink* it

but if you look pun e now
fragile, 'fraid o' e own shadow
but he tired, man, but he tired

he never get none o dem free trip to europe
dat i hear de civil service servants talk 'bout
he never get no pension from de people

when de dust in dat warehouse yard brek up e lung,
get on bad in e chess, cough wrackle e up like a steel
donkey, most kill e, you hear, before he did passin good forty

he never know what name pension nor compensation
for all dem mornins dat i hads was to get up 'fore six
to mek tea, slice bread, an scrape an butter de crackle

an place it before e, so he cud get down to town before open

they int give e no prize nor no piece o paper
for all de years dat e stannin' up there countin canefields;
buckley, vaucluse, mount all, fairfield, bissix, clifton hall, small . . .

de lorries slowly shippin up up de hill
de cane green, de cane ripe, de cane cut, de fields hot
cutlass sweet, cutlass sweat, cutlass singin

trash, windmill, crack, bubble o vat in de fac'try
load pun me head, load in de cart, de mill spinnin spinnin spinnin
syrup, liquor, blood o de fields, flood o' the ages

my ghost in your footstep, my eyes red in the hunger of your eyes
the lorries slowly shippin up up the hill
to the mill, to the fortress of bags in the warehouse, to the eyes

of my father

the merchant's clerk, the merchant's man, the merchant's prop/erty
black to his poor backra money
back to his poor backra psalm

Sam Lord

The lord is my shepherd
he created my black belly sheep

he maketh me to lie down in green pastures
where the spiders sleep

he leadeth me beside the still waters
lakes, green pond, constitution river, glitter bay

he leadeth me in the paths of righteousness for his name's sake
though i am dry as a cracked sculptor's mould

he restoreth my soul

yea, though i walk through the valley of the shadow of death
gullyroot, limegrove, lignum vitae

i will fear no eyevil: for thou are with me

ragged point at dream's morning
oistin town dripping to dust

thy rod and thy staff they comfort me
thou preparest a table before me in the presence of mine enemies

candle, book of confectionery that i will proudly bear
bell that i will break and pour its sound in the vèvè

breadnut: casket of my mother
plantain, mortar, slave song

and the grapefruit which is life which is love
which is death which is resurrection

skin of fire, pith of innocent air
pulp of flesh of freshest clear: gold volcano seed of earth

thou anointest my head with oil
halleluja

thy rod and thy staff no longer assault me
my cup of hands runneth over

surely goodness and mercy
francina and faith

shall follow me all the days of my life
and i will dwell in the house of the merchant for never

Bell

1

But my mother calls me back to her calm histories

2

parson replaced husband with the birth
of her second child/at the death
of the third

parson was mohammet in his pulpit
highland of moses up the curved and polished stair

parson spoke with the authority of heaven
above the dream of the choir

big black bible was a boulder that he rolled away each sunday
look, his glasses twinkle like the star of david:

parson so kind, parson so distant
parson come from so far away

you could only touch him with prayers

3

i have sinned, father
            against heaven and thy unholy maidservant

            the girl stink an she tongue is alive with fire
            she bag big an she fingers reckless

she is steal the silvers, rev'rent
an i hads was to tell her so

forgive me, father

4

pinafore, plaits, sunday school
an that yamvine boy, eddie branker, growin up tall an out/lorded

one sundee miss neblett did pick e to take up collection

an e did stann up there in de face o de class
wid de long jam bottle jam up in e hand' an he bare eye knees

an e creakin new shoes
an a shine pun e face like e was the arch-

angel uriel

5

> hear the pen/nies drop/in
> lissen while they fall
> ev/ry one for jee/sus
> he shall have them all
>
> drop/in drop/in drop/in drop/in
> hear those pen/nies fall
> ev/ry one for jee/sus
> he shall have them all

6

and it was like the lord himself
              should descend from heaven with a shout
                      with the voice of armageddon
                              and the trump of god

an i did love him so
               forgive me, father

the merchant own me husband
an me husband never home

                   forgive me, father

you think i did mout too much?
you think i did run im way?

7

i did dream o' dis house where we livin' now
how we cud own it
how i cudda put on a extra shed roof fuh de children
exten' de back garden, get a garage one day . . .

i did dream o' dis house as a palace where,
anytime you feel like it,
you cud stop off from whip from work from sunlip
an get a brown glass o' mauby or a batter o' breadfruit kukoo

as a place that did always tidy

clean cloth pun de tables
nuff glass pun de shelf
an de floorboards scrub up good good good
till de pains in me knees is the same

as de greenheart wood

i did dream o this place as a step forward outa de dark
outa de canefields uh come from

i dida want it to be a place
where i wouldn't feel shame to invite you

12

rev'rent

where yuh children coulda even drop in
to play ludo

i wasn't to know that he never would earn
enough from dat merchant to pay down de pay-down
before he did nearly half dead
as you see he dere now

i never did know, after he put dat ring pun muh finger
an i started breedin e children
i wudda have to get up an go out:
sellin shoes in de white people shop
to help enns meet in dis meat box

four mouts to feed
an de floor to clean when they throw up
all dat khaki to wash 'fore they walk off to school
an when they get back, mek dem tackle de form-
master home-

work; mek dem feel good when de boy
win a race or de girl get somethin
for sewin; mek dem snort
when uh hear dat dem lazy

i never did know when he start comin home
wid a wheeze: wid a cough: wid a stone in e chess
so he cud hardly breed, c'dear

when de duss dat e ketch in dat sun-
dayless wear-

house
brek e up like a stick

an pelt e down sick pun de grounn
when i did have was to knead e all night wid canadian healin oil

i never did know dat dat man he did work for
dat slack mister merchant wid dat black cattle hat

an e cravat: dat
poor backra rat

after all dem years
after all dem harvests o hogmeat an trash
in de canefields

after all dem soff bags o' sugar, reachin up to de dark o' de ceilin
after all dem books full o' figures an blames:
cart load, lorry load, spider load, headin:

after all dem thousands o' other men money dat pass thru e hands
after three hundred years in de hot sun

parson

you wudda think
wid e back brekkin up
wid e chess blackin up

dat dat man wudda call e
give e three hundred at least in he hann
fuh de years . . .

you know how i mean . . .?

not a cent
not a bline bloody cent
not even a dollar a year for de rock he was wrackin
not even a placket to help pay de rent

three hundred years come an three hundred years gone
an e sick an they tell im e dun
job pack up an finish an dun

so what e cud do but go wash e hanns
an pick up an put on e jacket an hat

so what e cud do
after all dem years . . .

quick step/chip step
as punctual as cat'olic bells . . .

an to know that he hads was to walk down de noon
down dat long windin day
to we home

8

is de bell, pastor john
leh me racket

is de bell, pastor john
leh me wreck it

till uh pour it sounn in de vèvè

Fever

And the stone wrinkled, cracked and gave birth to water

there was dream in my eye
there was vision of green
i sailed forward slowly into a movement of glass

everywhere there were lips: bubble and bud
and the crickets of birds

everywhere there were eyes: dressing me in robes
placing sandals under my feet, praising me

everywhere there were hands: building the temple

i was a door: opening
i was a window: looking onto a tree

and there was a landslide of memories

i grew softer and softer
until i could no longer remain still in that place

root upon wheels, i began my soft seam of descent
fold upon fold of cloth, strip upon strip of rumble

i moved downwards into the valley:
outhouse, train line, battlement of bridge i rolled away

but the dried grasses heard of my coming

pitiful and dim, they resisted erosion
but had already died the death of sticks and witches

they had lost the drum of beneficent sunlight
they had forgotten how to dance to cool and glint and trinkle

chained among weeds and brambles
they resembled my lost children:

those who had died: crossing
those who had had stakes stuck into their courage: refusing

those who had escaped into rum
into the long drag of the thighs of their women

who had let the hedges grow high, strangled with love-vine
who could only speak squeaking, with the voices of crickets.

now these lost saviours: djukas of marsh, maroons
of scar and cockpit country, boscoes of rock and thicket

prepare their roots for quicksilver
their backs for the cats of salvation

so that black sticks might sing
the thin antennae of stems receive the whisper of planets.

so i move down into the old watercourses

echo pebble trickle of worn stone
snaken voice of coral curling its own pattern to the sea

memory of foam, of fossil, eroded beaches high
above the eaten boulders of st philip

and i become dry pool: dead eye: frog's mudden jump: crab's
    skeletone:

hag raddled with sea salt: dumb
mouth: unmothered mother

though the stars dry away, waterwheels depart down the limestone
    and clay
and the bills must be paid for the food i can hardly afford

for the padlock, for the roof destroyed by the last season's fever
an i mussn't forget that i ax the teacher to stop in an see me
    tomorrow

Lix

1

Chalkstick the teacher

dreamer of sundaes
screamer of adjverbs, latin
ablutive clauses, mad-

rigal grace notes

tinkled his bicycle bell
years after the invention of the v-8 ford

it was 8.05 in the morning

mohammet
had come to my mother's black
mountain

and although the traffic was rushing towards the junctions like
    blood
clots: sugar pressure varicose vein: he knew

that he had many more lies to live

it was plain that perhaps, who knows,
he might become a senior master
one day, or even a min-

ister: *let me not think on it*: shakes-
pear? even his face, god wot,
in plaster of paris on one o' them lib'ry

shelves: *hmmmm*: long hair wig: me lod
the chief josstice: wreath-
ing the recitation for services rendered in ass-

isting the pupils of the un-
ready to win book fair prizes, blow
their brains up, demolish express

trains trans-
porting the virgin of guadeloupe, spin
tops, become nobel wize winners

he was already forty

married/un
married cow-

ard: living with
a woe-

man who dusted his chin
every born-

in
with baby's talcum pow-

der: hate-
ing her: need-

ing her daily as if
she was maid for the job

2

to build a nation of forked sticks
to kill the blade in those dark mahoe bodies

to iron the devil out of their pants
to see that they spit in tune

that they don't clap their hands, shake their heads, tap their feet
to the tam tom:

let there be no ting-ling no shak-shak
no drum

let them not stare from the whites of their eyes
at idols they have never forgotten

wear feathers
push bones through each others' congolese nostrils

but to have them neatly arraigned in squares:
packs packages the iron duke of wellington

the noble duke of york

as on the jesus ships of the faulked atlantic cross-
age: like cabbages, like sardine kings and queens

to have them honour this mean-
ness: knowing their place at the foot of the nation
backseat bus stop bellboy black

no jonah deep sea wailing driver
no daniels in the lions den
no martinlutherblazinpen

just charlie chalkstick the teacher

Occident

Chalkstick the teacher
dreamer of desk-

coteque and dais

crinkled his bicycle bell with the sound of ice in a bucket
and a pear flowed down the walls of his future

my mother heard and opened the door of the mountain
but he wouldn't come

in

at the window
then
widow

       with my father gone out among the hee-haws of donkeys
          and hawkers
       with his quick step: chip step
       and his greeting hand waving like if he mean no

       and his felt hat on like the back o the sun
       among cries and the fresh yellow energies of horse
       dung

this planter's puncher
looked in at her window
from his plantation into her plot

he did not know what pots were on her fire:
eddoes and yam in the kitchen

he did not know if there was pumpkin vine
running wild all over her backyard

22

if the gate-door creaked
if red crabs crawled in her rock

garden:
but he knew the mam looking at him:

squint-eye front-frown
keen glance made keener by glasses: gold

framed: the precious absent schoolboy sun
clutched to her ibo bosom

the teeth filed, ready for greeting,
the cool flat voice of her iron

getting hotter and hotter
as the galvanized roof of the red-shingled castle

crinkled and stretched in the daylight
its waves of tin going tick tick tick in the white sheet-shine

the kettle lips boiling to buse him, you hear,
if he didn't take care to be care-

ful, to be po-
lite, to be bow-

tie
to defuse her ticking stare

the fear he would not listen
showing where she did not smile:

that the boy would be a *lux*
occidente: her great light riding from the west

that even if she had to pick her way through sticks and broken
    pathways for
him

23

there would be the time, there would be the place, there would be
   the day . . .

she loved the sound of schoolbells
squares: triangles: hookey hockey matches

desks: gas chambers: forward march
it was the way the truth and the light

swords instead of ploughshares
heroes instead of helots

dreams where before the linen was rippled with nerves
exodus from house of bondage

into james bond in-bond shops and rats and cats and garbage.

so chalkstick smiled, accepting another black hostage
of verbs

Pig mornin

1

But my mother is down by the market bawlin' for fish:

scales, cavalee, the fret-saw tooth of the black
snapper

and there is seaweed

worries ripple her brow
like evening wind upon water

spiders make patterns in her mind

her voice on the telephone
is a dry echo out of a shell

her knife scrapes the rake of the chubbs
and the sparks of their dead sea fires fly

the life-gold rings: the chipped enamel bowl

> her husband out there on the plantation
> her children locked up into their cell

> blocks of school and a knock
> upon the cracked door

> redwood: a knob: grey panels: jalousies

> *what price de fish hay!*
> baskets breeze skillets clinks

> man with a peaked cap out there among the lilies
> jack stock: the debt collector

25

2

so what you want, jock?

memory of crack and hurricane
black belt of smoke, judos of killer
flies: bulldozer: pencil: howl: check-

off

fifteen dollars an thirty-five cents
where de fish!

harsh voices: soft question

doan tell me you isn't remember again
bolts, nails, 12 saws o' lumber

kingfish, mullets, some-
body got shark but i isn't want shark

rent owin' pun two o de shop

but why you is want to stretch me strait out pun de wrack
o de mornin so early for, man? i int even sweep

de yard yet. w'as happen to you: you wife leak you?

3

i drivin de bus when de accident happen
two schoolchildrens dead an i hobblin bout
pushin dis new-

fangle mfp floor-
ide for a star-
spangle amurican firm:

panga an pepsident/fit for de president
so smile de smile of de yale
carnegie unhesitant resident

who to void an avoid industrial
was'e is ube de pas'e clear-
fully

squeezin de white people worm from de tube.
so smile de smile of de man who
all de hoof of e head mash out in de crash

an e earin teef gone an glass
brekkin
and de steel o de bus frame squeel-

in out like a pig gwine to market an start bennin up like a vwww
as if it did mek out a tinnin

an in front o me eyes is
little black dots like is weebles
in rice you is pick wid you hann from shop-paper

since den i int holdin a job till i lannin dis one
from de warehouse man by de corner:
debt collectin: pickin up sticks

but is you an miss
porrige an de one they call-

in molasses gertseen an dat
oughtna greenidge

who live in de new flat roof house in de ivy
an buyin up all o' dem new flashion blouses

who givin me all o dis trouble. is
fifteen dollars an thirty-five cents

4

an de eye of de door
knob won't open itself to the sun

light: an de dark o' de door
can't open it heart to the poor

an if uh doan get it dis morn-
in: *look love uh got dese bananas fuh you:*

is goin' be de law
an de larr o de lawyer

bull pessle trailin it ash
in de air

cause you losin dis house
or i lossin dis job

when crappau eat louse
he leff grass fuh de dog

you losin dis house
or i hollerin hog

cause de eccky beccky tief
who owin me head

will spit in me face
where i isn't got teef

an to loss dis space
is to lay down dead

i sorry/you sorry
i sow what you grow

but when de cock crow
you know how it go

so you losin dis house
or i lossin dis job

when crappau eat louse
he leff grass`fuh de dog

5

so my mother walks on beaten stones
on childhood steps across the river

she did not make sheep
in the early morning

she is not a fisherman
striding at dawn

she is not god
the stonebreaker

or a washer-
woman whitening her

boulders from sleep

she is smaller than these
she has become greater than these

she is like a nut-
meg grater: rough

and aromatic:
you may stuff

her into your pocket:
she will rock

you back under a sudden
stagger of rain.

29

she knows that the sky is blue
because the loam is there

she watches the sea's whisper
with love, because she will always walk

on cavernous limestone. she smiles
at jack strap now because she is stronger

than pencil or pen, book bulldozer or pay-
off: because she is soft-

er now than his jeer, than his jibe, than his jail.

alone in her house, filled with the sound of leaves
and the shudders of lilies, scoured

by the acid of eels, she opens her clip-
top red and white purse: bead-

ed all over: some lost, others slack:
the metal clicks slightly worn, rusted and bent:

and pays him his dollars and dirty-five cents.

Tear or pear shape

Is this why there are no rivers running in my island
why you see dry water courses if you follow the shape of the
    bramble
the curve of the slow growing green, the sunken gums of the parish
why you remember only its history of pebbles?

for how can water flow from rock
when the dust blinds the dream of the shocked eye
how can cool silver break from coral limestone
when no wind of rain breaks in upon our prophecies

how can there be a carved trail
when schools teach their children blasphemies:
the blasphemy that the word is law when spoken by an english
    engineer
that our teaching must reflect these verities

the boy/stood on/the burn/in deck
whence all/but he /had

flowered

dead river courses: dry causes
the leaves of the land eaten by tourists

my mother's vision blocked by bricks and cement blacks

leak of cool from the grass
from the glass of thirst

in her throat
          and her children

          wearing dark glasses
          hearing aids

leaning on wine

on the dark sibyls of asia minor
on the flat bergs of western ontario

build houses bigger than she has need for
and lock her out of them

chip chapels where they will worship
the winking gods of electron

and disc jockey her into them

carve pools where there is no surface of whales
where all is blue and cool and tear shaped

II

NIGHTWASH

Miss Own

1

Selling calico cloth on the mercantile shame-
rock, was one way of keeping her body and soul-seam together
surrounded by round-shouldered backras on broad street
by cold-shouldered jews on milk

market

in the dark ghetto store
the bolt of cloth tugged, turned, revolved upon its wooden thunder

revealing rivers of green beige and muslin
lightnings of foreigner factories, bourgs

sign a bill here

and the storewalker
plodding prodding

        indentured to the merchant's law
        the merchant's whip
        the merchant's weakly pay

comes

on his own flat foot to
sign the bill here
figures snakes and foxes

for some pampered child's penthouse apartment high above new
   york
listening, on her wheel of self-indulgent sorrow
to roberta flack

while our barrow boy calls

rags ole rags: cloze ole cloze
got any ole bottles today?

she sippin she drink
an i slippin out into de heat o de sun
to buy what me scrape from she barrel

2

selling half-sole shoes in the leather
department, was another good way of keeping her body and soul-
    seam together

toes: scorn: instep: honeycomb of boxes: stretch
up: pull down: put down: open

the tanneries of morocco, of algeciras, sokoto, of boot
leg lacquered italy: buffalo and cow horn rumbling

into the stockyards of styx of chicago
abattoirs of spout and thunder: sloped slaughterhouses of the
    chamois studded bronx:

cries calls clanks butchers' halls' bulls' knives stretching up: pulling down: putting down: open-

ing up the blood of the in-
growing toe-nail: worship of creak and spine

ache

3

for the shoe is a safe cottage to the illiterate peasant
needing light, running water, the indestructible plastic of the soft
    ill
lit/erate present

sign a bill here

and she kneels before the altar of the golden calf
altering its tip and instep
keeping body an soul-seam together

and the merchant smiles, lost in his founderies
setting out on his barefooted pilgrimage
across the inverterate prairies

Horse weebles

Sellin biscuit an sawlfish in de plantation shop at pie
corner, was another good way of keepin she body an soul-seam
   together

she got she plot of cane, she cow, she fifteen pigeons in a coop,
razzle-neck fool-hens, a rhode islan' cocklin,
yam, pumpkin, okro, sweet
potato, green pea bush

there is lard ile in de larder
an shark ile for the children's colds
there is easin' ile for crusty locks
and castor oil with lime or salt or sugar for extreme
distress, and candle grease for sea-egg pricks an chiggoes

but she sells in the plantation shop at pie corner, hoping to make
   enns meet.

from she left school, taking up sewing since she was fourteen,
bringin forth myrtle, den eggbert, den
sammy an redsin de twin wuns

not a sarradee come you cahn fine she in there after 'leven o'clock
heat risin: smokin hi'sin' outside: blackbirds hidin from sun
white: weighin out flour, choppin up salt beef, countin out biscuit

shovellin
oat flake out o' de tin while she
frettin

evenin' miss
evvy, miss
maisie, miss
maud, olive

how you? how
you, eveie, chile?
you tek dat miraculous bush
fuh de trouble you tell me about?

de cornmeal flour is flow thru she fingers like time
self, me chile

the saltfish barrel is dark like a well an is broaden out to a lake
   at de bottom
where de swink is splash into slippery conger-eels

the crystal sugar is shine like stars that does twinkle into de dark
o' de akee tree

but you tek
it?

ev'ry night 'fore uh gets
into bed.

uh bet-
'cha feelin less
poorly a'ready!

i int know, pearlie,
man, any-
way, de body int dead.

no man, you even lookin
more hearty!

a'ready?
then all uh kin say
an uh say it agen:
we got to thank god
fuh small mercies

an she is dream of tears of stone
of dark meroë water lapping at the centre of the world

but then is cries an hungry faces: children
who can hardly shit: tin bones of ancient skeletones

the planter's robber's waggon wheels and whips
and she trapped in within her rusting canepiece plot.

so sar'dee nights when you hearin de shout
mister greedyman boltin he bars cross de gate
de pump-up glass lamp soon outin out

she is dust off she hanns
put back de rounn biscuit lid pun de barrel
help lock stock and socket de shop

collect what little they give she in small
change, handin back what she owe pun de frock

goin slowly down in de winks o de dark
to de half lot o' lann dat she callin a home

an not sayin a word to a soul what she see what she dream what
she own

Woo/Dove

1

Who calls the lightning down
to this tilted cracked fragmented landscape
who engineers the landslide

makes the trees walk, the roads disappear over the howl of night
who leaks the soil out, staining the rock of my fingers
who crushes it soft into putty to bitters to clay

these cobb skinned potters have deserted their ancient endeavours
their kilns are uncovered: their crafty fingers fear shadows
their bellows are bloated with mildew and wheezy with hidden
    holes

their goats nibble grass to the very edge of disaster
where wriggles a ragget of green
the sun is sucked into boulder and brown

drifting dust. the children of life here
are brambles: bright eyed like lizards or birds
as quick and as hungry as twittered to wind as the trashes

the garbage has stretched its thick lips from the city
it kisses the village with litter
it whispers

canadian cornfields of plastic to stephanie
where her distant father eats well:
electrical canefields: niagara falling:

swords ploughshares and phosphates:
the branches and roots of her body
are chalk with the saltlicks of dew

41

there is blue between cactus and claws
of the ocean: sea-island cotton cracks out of her cinder and shell,
the rocks on the hill have been tuned to black harps by the long

seaswell

2

but what she go do
jess pickin she mind wid she fingers
scatterin blackbirds outa de grass

an watchin dem climb into bastards

is nine good years since she father slip outa dis desert
wid a whole set o niggers: he head puff up like a powder puff

in de esquimo street he still standin up
in in de city o montreal.
that is all

de man ever senn we:

one brown tinted picture from canada dry
not a bline starvin penny
half dollar or crew cut american cent

an is nine good years since e leff we

3

so what she go do
three years now she was tekkin
commercial down at de modern, mekkin

shorthan' while she learnin to type
but she dear-aunt done dead
de one who did prayin de school

fees

she cud clip an sew
bleach starch an i: ron out cloze
try she hann at conkey or pone

sell cherry or duncks by de road
side: go to town as a clerkess
stannin up all day in she stockin an pride

or lettin de fat crawl up outa she back-
slide like dem sittin-down cashier in cheap-
side: clink-

in people good money into de till
till dem black ass turn blue
and for who

4

so come darlin chile
the man want
the man want to meet
the man want to meet you too much

you int see how he glad?
the man want to tuh
the man want to touch
say he want to teach you de lancers

wuh dah? de man musse mad, bo!

jess sweet you too bad
say he want you to dance
say he feel he cud chance it
wid you

43

it int hard, leh me tell you
jess sad
so come darlin chile
leh me tell he you ready you steady you go

Hex

1

So she sings of streams
that are a-glutter with boulders

of rocks that have not forgotten
their ancestry of iron

she quarrels like the dry seeds of the lotus rattle

she rattles like dry tamarind pods
like shak shaks

she shakes
and her tongue climbs a hill of dry consonants

she is alpha
she is omega
she is happy

it is not failure that disturbs her:
she dreams and interprets her dreams

it is not crack of faith that disturbs her
she has seen too many ghosts

it is not fear:
for she is always alone

2

but she weepeth long into the night
white trail of salt is there upon her cheek
among her loves, there is none left to comfort her

all her friends, ladies of fashion
parsons of bibles of temper, beggars who hurled stones
into the mangrove stores
all have dealt treacherously with her
her feet know quicksand
her steps know the sough of despond
the pathways, the doors, the jealousy windows,

outlooks of uncertain knowledge:
eyes peep glint steel:
these are now certainly enemies
and because her inheritance is swallowed by strangers:
her houses, her beaches, the views of her landscape
from which the youngsters sap milk
are turned over to tourists: to terrorists:
she mothers us as if we were orphans and fatherless
as if she were a witch or a widow of prophets.
all the peaks, the promontories, the coves, the glitter

bays of her body have been turned into money
the grass ploughed up and fed into mortar of houses
for master for mister for massa for mortal baas
her sands are now owned by the minister midas
and have been burned into careful gold brochures
the leaves of her trees are now printed in amsterdam
her breadfruit is sold into foreigner factories
and returned to her sons wrapped up in tins to be eaten as chips
and the lips of the bankers smile as they rip her children to debts
there is more weed than food in the island

3

so she sits, bandana ikon

stool in the corner
that cool stone in the backyard
that flat rock underneath the cotton tree
that rocking chair on the enslaved verandah

black sycorax my mother

she is as young as the pouis
as ancient as dead leaves
she will outlast the present season's thunder
the ovens of august

and the september's breath of hurricanes;
and when the wind from the east brings dust,
brings crack, brings flowers,
she will begin to creak and give the dry rot meaning

she will remember the floorboards of a cabin
how there was a grave there
where she buried her children
their skin drilled to screams like the soft of guavas by the flicker
    of birds

she will remember the eyes
sinking into the night of dead water
cries of flame when there was gun-
fire, gong beat and the cripple footsteps running from the tribe

she wears on her wrist the shadow of the chain
history of flesh
written by whip of torture
legacy of bribe

from the sicknesses of the plantation
she gathers sticks
gutters them to fashion pipes flutes siphons
rambles of herbs she touches and sniffs

offering them prayers and names:
mint nunu kema-weed shamar
pem-pem piaba fall-down-bush
and she crumples words into curses:

4

let unhappiness come
let unhappiness come
my face strikes a match of darkness

scrape for your itches
crack for your giddy spell
gutter and out for your blindness

let unhappiness come
let unhappiness come
work not for your mother

cry not for your father
let unhappiness come
may you steal crusts of bread

may you nibble the neighbour's meat
curdle his milk
melt his oxen hoof down to glue

if you join a circle: break it

if the monkey is cool
tang of clay in the pool
water: break it

if the baby will sleep, fist
curled, thumb in the mouth: dribbling happiness
wake it wake it

even where the plague dog lies with his black tongue
    laughing lapping
you must wake it wake it wake it

if you see white
it will not be the white clay of celebration

if you see red
it will not be the elders approaching

for the whipped slave
cannot love you

the split back
ripped black of the animal from its pack
of hearts cannot love you

the broken lives, broken eyes
shattered syllables of leaves
cannot love you

even though my wound beats with your christ's wrist

may unhappiness come
may unhappiness come
blasting the roots and branches

may unhappiness come
may unhappiness come
halting the harvest

may you trip your foot up on wednesday
may your mirror shatter on sunday

i will hoot upon your head with owls and john crows
i will trap your legs with scorpions and blisters

let unhappiness come
let unhappiness come
let unhappiness come

my face is towards the darkness where our voices are not
   one

5

But the children, locked away in their factories of schools
know nothing of these matters
they can change nothing that is theirs/not theirs

they eat paper, they spit out half-chewed words
they burn king alfred's cakes
but cannot help with the housework

bucket on head of water they say no to
sweeping the yard they will not undertake
milking the goat is impossible

they learn to smile with keats and milton
but forget lizzie and joe
they sing men of harlech
but know nothing of the men who marched

from congo rock
from belleplaine
from boscobelle
from hothersal turning

calling for rifles: not smatters
calling for bread: not highly bibles
calling for shillings won't break on their teeth into crack into
    broken clay

for the children know nothing in their prisons
except how to praise god, honour the king
and betray their own country

they will grow up to be good teachers
soft spreading doctors, lawyers, political liars
builders of lyrical bricks along the sandy shores of atlantis

other men will come bringing flowers, shadows, slaughters
other men will revive the strangled loves of their daughters

for the mind is dry
where there are no rivers

the sky of hope shines high with barren metal
where there are no watercourses

i struggle through the silver thorn
and cannot find the pool

Milkweed

1

But my father has gone out on the plantation
he used to make us windmills
spinnakers of trash when the crack of cane was in the air

the brown stalks wrinkled and curled in the wind like scarecrows
    of orange angels
and butterflies flickered as the clipped straw clicked
on its pin as it picked up speed

but for years he has brought us nothing
for years he has told us nothing
his verbs shut tight on his briar

while my mother watches him go
with his cap and his limp and his skillet of soup
and we never look at his hands

2

look at his hands:
cactus cracked, pricked,
worn smooth by the hoe,
limestone soil's colour:
he has lost three fingers
of his left hand falling
asleep at the mill:
the black crushing grin
of the iron tooth'd ratchets
grinding the farley hill cane
have eaten him lame
and no one is to blame

the crunched bone was juicy
to the iron: there was no difference
between his knuckle joints
and ratoon shoots: the soil
receives the liquor with cool flutes:
three fingers are not even worth a stick
of cane: the blood
mix does not show, the star-
gaze crystal sugar shines
no brighter for the cripple blow:
and nothing more to show
for thirty years' spine

curving labour in clear
rain, glass eyed, coming off
the sea, fattening up the mud
in the valleys, cours-
ing down hillsides, caus-
ing the toil of the deep,
well-laid roots, gripping soil,
to come steadily loose, junction and joint
between shoot and its flower to be made nonsense of:
and the shame the shame the shame-
lessness of it all: the name-
less days in the burnt cane-

fields without love: crack of its
loud trash, spinn-
ing ashes, wrack
of salt odour that will not free
his throat: the cutlass falling, fall-
ing: sweat, grit between fingers,
chigga hatching its sweet nest
of pain in his toe
and now this and now this:
an old man, prickled to sleep by the weather, his labour,
losing his hands . . .

Valient

1

But the man who possesses us all
who has broken the heart of my father's hands

who shits in the great house
surrounded by ticks, by collocks, by the clicking calendars of peals

who possesses the mountain where the water peels out from the
   rock
and the river begins

who watches the breeze on the hill
signalled by semaphore windmills

who tunes in to all the noises we make:
cough and barrak, clankton of rivets, sizzle of kettle and leaves

who switches on thunder: waterfalling of engines that make our
   rooms shake
who leeches on to the black

electrical pips of our sisters
yet teaches his silversnout wolves how to murder

barefooted work-
men, tracked by the sweat of their arm-

pits:
doan like we at all

2

he is come from away, i hear maisie say
(she is work near de dogs an de engines)

an is worship a god who is move in de clouds wid moses an dem
when they went up into de mountains to pray

who was transfigured, bread and buried: who ascended into hell
and the nex day rose agen from de dead wid i clot

and clambered up into the churchbells:
ev'ry sundee since then you kin hear how he ringin

i hear maisie say

he is walk through the portals: woodcarved, shiney wid linseed
in de long white dress that sophie is wash wid she hanns

an stamp stamp stamp wid de little black coalpot i:ron she got
till ev'ry t'read stretch out an straight

an de starch pun it shine like de cheek o de moon

then foldin three notes rounn a fifty cent piece
(he cudda more than afford it)

an slippin it into de pocket o cloth
de deacon is put pun a stick an push cross de pew

IHS

embroider upon it
(is pretenn uh doan see it since poor me one cahn really afford it)

he is sink like a umman down pun e knees
cryin out loud like e catchin de spirit

holee holee holee ee nominee

i inn know what it mean: uh cahn mane it
but maisie say that he buyin ark-angels

swords an a burnin bush: like when adam pitch outa even

55

Nametracks

1

But

muh
muh
muh
me mudda
mud
black fat
soft fat man-
ure

kukoo
cook-
in pot herb
wollaboa wood
eve-
ning time smoke
sleep
sleep
rest

2

muh
muh
me muddah
mud
doan like what she see
she doan like e
she doan like e at all
she doan light e
she is wa/wa/wash she is watch e

she is spit right into he all-seein eye
that she draw wid she toe pun de grounn

an she spite/in an spite/in
she spite/in an spitt/in
she curses upon him
wid de sharkest toot o she tongue

3

the man who possesses us all
who brek de heart o she husbann hann
who wreck de lann o me faddah
doan possess we at all, she is tell muh

e di go
e go di
e go dead

she is tell muh

e go day
e go dog
e go die

she is tell muh

ma ma ma: she is tell muh
ma ma *man*: she is tell muh

ma ma *man*: she is tell muh

say *man*: she is tell muh
say *man*: she is tell muh

say *man*
say *manding*
say *mandingo*

4

but

ogrady says
say i
say i

not me
not man
not muddah

i

say
i
ogrady says

say
i
not

eye

globe
seeing word
blue priest
green voodoo doctor

say

i
am your world

you must not
break

it: quick
ogrady says

say
stick

say
dog

say
sick

say
good

say
god

say
wick

ogrady says

say
whip

say

i
ogrady says
say

i
say
i

say
i
ogrady says

say
aei

5

but

me muh
me muh
mud
me mudda

brek
de word
she eat it like cheese
like curl'd milk
like yellow bread

an she te an she teach an she teach mih

dat de worl' risin in de yeast
wid red wid cloud wid mornin mist
wid de eye: ron of birds

6

but

look
ogrady says

look lock
ogrady says

lock bar bolt rivet
and throw away the prison

say lack
ogrady says

say key
ogrady says

key quai kaie sky
ogrady says

an darken your derision

say i
ogrady says

say i
say i
say ice

ogrady says

not cool
ogrady says

say kill

not keel
ogrady says

say ship
say whip

not sheep
ogrady says

say kill

sails
future wrack
plantations greening

say scream
ogrady says

eye
cannot dream

ogrady says

say hit
say hot
say pot

say rot
ogrady says

say rat

say right
say white
say wrong

say strong
ogrady says

not song

say trip
say trap
say sit

ogrady says
say shit

say pain
say blame
say cane

say name
ogrady says

not me
not muh
not mudda

drain

ogrady says
say

name

say run
ogrady says
say shame

say sun
say flame
say bramble

i come
ogrady says

to strangle
you maim
in de grounn

7
but

muh
muh
mud
me mudda

coo
like she coo
like she cook
an she cumya to me pun de grounn

like she lik mih

like she lik me wid grease like she grease mih
she cum to me years like de yess off a leaf
an she issper
she cum to me years and she purr like a puss and she essssper

she lisper to me dat me name what me name
dat me name is me main an it am is me own an lion eye mane
dat whinner men tek you an ame, dem is nomminit diff'rent an nan
so mandingo she yessper you nam

8

ku late
cries ogrady
high year what she yell yuh
an i tekkin you number down on i plate
mek i tell yuh

i learn
says ograde
what she bell yuh

but i doan want no oo-
ma nor congolese mudda
to hell i in here
leh me quell yuh

so is i
says ogrady
say i

says ogrady
say i

says ogrady

but eye bline to de worl'
where you see mih,
cahn seh what me see when you say mih

so quick
says ogrady
say stick

says ogrady

stick likkin an warrikin trix
leff a crik in me nek an ogrady stick brek

but wot about wog, stars shoutin ogrady
wow wow wow wog, hows ogrady

dog dark in e bark but doan bite mih, ogrady
wog lark

but i sharp, says ogrady
say sick or i run a stark
plimpler or root in ya stomache
an you slippin an yella an hobble

tomb ich trouble, ogrady
when you kick me up me still tickin

so whip, says ogrady
shay whip, says ogrady
clip a nigger switch from de tamarind tree
an i wreck you in two when i weddy

but it red off me back an it rocket
black up an lack it doan like you ogrady

so i keel you (ogrady)
i diggin you coffin blox black in de brown
an i livvin you dead in de grounn

9

but me head hard ogrady
an me doan give a damm

me back to me belly
an me dun dead a'ready

back to back belly to belly
dun dung dead in de grounn

10

an

e

nomminit
nomminit
nomminit

an

e

nomminit
nomminit
nomminit

lame me black
lame me blue
lame me poopapadoo

lame me nig
lame me nog
lame me boobabaloo

but he never know what me
  main

an

e

nomminit
nomminit
nomminit

an

e

nomminit
nomminit
nomminit

but e nevver maim what me
  mudda me name
an e nevver nyam what me
  mane

11

back to back belly`to belly
uh doan give a damm

uh dun dead a'ready

back to back belly to belly
dun dung dead in de grounn . . .

III

TUK

Dais

1

Um was a little black dog
bow-leg waggle-tail whipper-snapper
wid nuff plenty snuff colour fleas

ann feedin it pap in de kitchen

judge jackson was out
gone for de day dung to pleasant hall
but for all you know by now he in town
out by de churchwall pun mason hall street

or clickin' up sticks in de folly

mistress jackson home, doh
an miss speckle-face varney dat doan say a ting
an miss betty:

nine years ole where de trouble start

2

ever see a cat dat does rub up it furr pun yuh foot
nice nice nice: soff an purr
when um feel like it?

ever see a cat dat does peel it purr pun yuh foot
when it feel
like it: and den when it dun: when it dun rub you dung

de chat gone:
gone long like if it doan know you
from adam or even ezekiel?

betty so

3

nine year ole betty jackson get outta she bed an nine o'clock strikin
mistress jackson she mudda is get up at twelve
when de face o de daylight start fight-

in it shadow:
she gettin on now
she nerve shallow

cock-a-doogle crow got to grow
into hee-haw bray o de donkey
fore de wood say flax an you know she unshatter she shutter

4

but betty up early
an bo
is trouble she shellin

nevva trouble trouble
true
till trouble trouble you

smood pebble o tongue in she mout and she yarnin
all dem holes hatchin outta she mout: she int want dem:
she even beg ann for a chawstick to chew wit'

an she brushin she teet and she garglin:
dem larrnin:
she get up an nevva say marnin

5

ann sittin dung dere in de half open door light
feelin cumfie an cool pun she bottsie
she face half shadow an happy

bird songs touchin de bread crumbs she got in de bucket dere
    soakin in milk
de doctor bird visit de hibiscus tree
and de hoverin green of it wing in ann eye

when it move
de light of it brilliant wash up pun de silk o she skin
like sheer-water

6

ann feedin de puppy

got it cotch in she lap wid it head in de bucket
when *bap*
betty mek one grab at de lil pappy: *so*

an de puppy-head turn rounn an *whelpit*

bett rip back she hann as if he did bite it
an nearly fall over ann foot pun de floor

she cahn help it

she head hit de door an de door handle rattle
an de doctor bird back backin quick quick outa de flowers an gone

not a sparrowbird song in de t'icket

7

it go so:

bett stann by de door and she rubbin she nobbit
movin she mout like she chewin dry
stick: den leggo one turruble kick at ann head

me see how she foot bottom dutty

ann sideways she head from de knock o dat blow
an she rock back quick before betty cud know
and drive one butt in she backside

look me crosses now nuh
look de trouble me see
de two o dem mekkin one big pappyshow

8

ann quiet an long
you cud see how she fingers
like splints or like splinters

how she natty head dred
so is ketch ev'ry hook
an eye in de nettle an grass o' de hickey

how she neck stem rising up cool an vase from she breast-
bone
how she shoulder blades balancin quiet an straight like is brass
scales

dat she growin up strong

9

betty wrong

she know in she poor backra heart dat she wrong
but she got she two hanns up pun she hip
and she mout pout out like a nayga

what a way she larnin, me whisper

nine knobble knee years growin up from de grounn
an a'ready she know how to skiffle an tack
wrapple roun in de wind to get what she wish when she want

it

cahn beat ann she self
but she self goin to get ann a beat-
in: you watch

10

it:

you drownin de dawg in de liquor, man, ann

do what? hook back ann
mekkin to gi' she a jook wid she elbow

i int got needa dog in no lappid-face pap
an you know it, you becky-face nigga

ann custom to kick an scratch in dis place
jack johnson goin breed an born from she waise
he goin carry on bad an mash up you face

71

11

you see, betty say
you see what she say?
who you callin a nigga you nayga

and she squeeze up she dry water pas'e like a wash-rag an cryin

12

what a way dem is mek we burn in we black-
ness: what a way dem is trouble me see

maaa: betty bawl out: she face makin *waaa*
ann tellin a story out hey pun me

she doan feed de dawg, jook she hann in i back
and say dat i favor a nigga

Nights

1

Scratchin she thighs and de sides o she belly
she head stickin outta she nightgown like duppy
mistress jackson open she mout an begin:

you fuhgettin youself you lil senseh-head hetty
i tell you a'ready doan mess wid miss betty
jess heiss dat pappy dawg beck in you lep
fore i swim you in licks wid dis catty

hear ann:

me feed it a'ready mish jackson an dun
look how de dog belly fum: it tann tum

2

you yellin at i, you saucer face ninny
you tryin to tell i i doan know de heat of i own pappy dawg
an it mout when it finish an done?
tek it up, mek i tell you, or i skin you like skim milk or scum

ann cut she eye baad
like she doan know she place
an she pout out she mout like a nayga

she grab up de poo where it splat pun de floor
but she choopse up she toot like you mout rippin clot
and de clot was mish jackson face

3

ann only twelve years:
if you look pun de smood at de side o she face
you cud see it

down dere in de pool o she neck
watch out how dem feinty lines crossin de cool like a cobweb an ketchin de light when she stretchin

but under she dress
all up an dung she back and she backside
c'dear, all dung de back o she foot

look how she have to hop pun she side-
step; how
de ankle bones twist

how de stock marks lock in she flesh

you see how she spine?
all dem fine bones chip up an jigg like a grater
look how she knucks flatten an raff

under she half-rip slip-cotton dress
she skin strike up an down like a razor
she belly an tie all welt up an silver

like she fright in a cage wid a tyger

4

how much am i bid?

nan
nan
nan

anan

74

never a man

nam

i see bugles shields gunmetal unglints
guttering eagles coming to meet me

i hear the coiner's voice of the fat auctioneer
the pulpit his strumpet and chair

making meat of god's wonders
her neck the globes of her ear and her lightning

how much am i bid?

do i hear amber
do i hear blue
do i hear mambo
do i hear you

four five sex and a live tv shew

do i jook
do i cook
do i hook

onto you

flushing you out with my soap flakes and fire
rustling you out with my germ heat and wire

do i wear
do i wear
so i weary you down

how steep
can you hide
can you hide me

how weep
can you bribe me
how cry am i bid?

nan
nan
nan

anan

never a nam

gnashlish

Cherries

1

So when the hammers of the witnesses of heaven are raised all
    together
up yonder

there will be dumbness in the choir tonight

when the voices are raised all together
black kites flying on what should be a holiday

there will be silence in the cathedral

a woman loves a man

she will lick the sweat from his forehead
she will walk miles to see him
and wait for him by the corner

she will bear his children loudly

upon the earth is firm foot
toes searching the top-soil
gripping

the instep, the angles of knub, heel and ankle
are grey with the roads
with the long hypodermics of noon

the dress tucks itself over the black buttocks
into the suction of thighs
the hip is a scythe
grass growling along the hillside

she will bend forward with the hoe: *huh*
and the gravel will answer her: *so*

she will swing upward with the hoe: *huh*
and the bones of the plantation will come ringing to meet her: *so*
her sweat will water the onions and the shaddock and the wild
   thyme

she will bear his children proudly

but when he turns sour on her
scowling, wiping her face with his anger
stiffening his spine beside her on the bed
not caressing her curves with eye-

lash or word or jook of the elbow
she will curdle like milk
the bones of the plantation will come ringing to meet her: *so*
the bucket will rattle in the morning at the stan'pipe

but there will be no water
the skillet will rattle at midday
but there will be no milk
she will become the mother of bastards

2

when the hammers are raised all together
rows of iron teeth swinging down: *huh*

there will be dumbness in the choir tonight

when the voices are raised all together
black fists gathering storm on what is not
a holiday

there will be silence in the cathedral

the light will fall through pains of glass
on broken stone

78

on steps that can go no father
on love alive bleeding on its thorns

when a woman loves a man
when a man naddent

3

if there are ways of saying yes
i do not know them

if there are dreams
i cannot recall them to the light

if there is rage
it is cool cinder

in the heat of the day
i swear i will sweat no more

knife, bill-hook, sweet bramble
i will burn in my bush of screams

hoe: i will work
      root, mud, marl, burden

needle: i will sew
      thread, stitch, embroidered image

jesus: i will serve thee
      knee, copper, rain falling from heaviest heaven of storm

but i will drink you no more
torch you no more
sweaten you out on the lumps of the mattress no longer

the hoe will stand in the corner by the backdoor
cane flowers will flicker with rainflies
but there will be no crop-over songs

the fields will grow green soundlessly
the roots will fatten until they burst
and then they will fatten again until they burst

but there will be no kukoo or okro or jug

the needle will grow rusty in the cloth:
pin, pinch of thread, thimble:
it will make no silver track and tremble far into the night

no dress will take shape over my head
slipping down like water over my naked breasts

the seats of the chapel will remain empty
the wicks burning at altar till daybreak
fattened by shadows and moths

your foetus i will poison
dark dark mollusc
spinach, susum, suck-de-well-dry bush

the child still fish, still lizard,
wrinkled gill and croaking gizzard

i will destroy: blinding the eyeballs
pulling out the flag of its tongue by the shreds
ripping open the egg of its skull with sunless manchioneal blisters

i will carry the wet twitching rag
bearing your face, conveying your futureless race
in its burst bag of balls to your doorstep

maaaa: it will cry
and the windows will be pulled down tight against the wind

meeowww: it will howl
and a black dog will go prowling past the dripping pit latrines

and when the moon is a wild
flower falling through cloud, from patch to shade you will see it

once our child, our toil of touch, our sharing
sitting under the sandbox tree, smiling smiling

slipping its plate of bleed

4

these images of love i leave you
when i no longer need you

man, manwart, manimal

Prayer

1

And after that
      these few prayers following
      all devoutly kneeling
      she remembering

and the minister
      white cassock, black flock
      pronouncing
      in a voice loud and doddering

shall say
      the lord be with you
      and with thy spirit

      bells incense censer swinging

let us prayer

      lord have mercy upon us
      christ have mercy upon us
      lord have mercy upon us

kneeling

      our father which art in

kilimanjaro

      hallowed be thy

nyam

      thy kingdom come
      thy will be done
      in earth as it is

dark dark dark

her feet tapp/ing tapp/ing tapp/ing
return/ing her to her chair in the corner
under the creakings of crows

    give us this day our dearly bread

    subtle street
    nelson street
    lightfoot lane

    in the blue
    in the eye
    in the peril of the cane

    and forgive us our trespasses

cup
cool of the cotton bowl
shank of the clanking loom

    as we forgive them that trespass against us

look, i stretch out this prayer
and it snaps like a mined thread against me
my thoughts collapse without their cornerstones of words
i rust at the corneas where there should have been salt

    and lead us not into temptation

sails cannot hold wind
drums cannot remember annunciations
dawn will not be able to hoist festivals
bringing the steelband men over the river in wooden ferries

how will i know that that click of camera, camel-
humped mohammet

will not convert you from island to islam
pebble to perfect catapult

but deliver us from wee/vil

for thine is the kingdom
the power and the glory
for ever and ever

amen

2

then the priest standing up shall say

i cannot live on olives

they have been brought by strange smiling brown skinned
    merchants
who smell of disaster

o lord have mercy upon us
curist have mercy upon us
lord have mercy upon us

i desire the yams of ibadan
the wool of the lambs shorn by the lake shores of the luo

o lord
shave thy people
and mercifully hear us when we call upon thee
o lord

yet the yam climbs fist over fist up its green flag-
pole and is a discotheque of silver worms:
the god eating its own mouth of flashing light
of dribble dust and rockstone

the old man with his carrion bag
uncle macoute

   endure thy ministers with righteousness

with his head of eyes closed
rows of organ teeth smiling smiling

gnashing in combat with the knife

cracking the necklace of my skull
my broken nose of ecstasy

   o lord save thy king/doom . . .

3

my mother blazes forth to these from faithless night

Moth air

But today she comes in
boy me feet heavy

de tiredness passin
like waterclouds carryin

rain: varicose veins sugar:

the room is a dark pool
the round table's epergne

drifts towards her
seaweed of carpet

shadows of pictures on the wall
the dark clouds carrying rain

nobody home?
she hears her throat

ask its whisper. silence
from the kitchen: clash

pots, water doze
and nozzle, imperial

soup tureen. silence
from the backroom: rust-

less newspapers, shopp-
ing bags filling with musk

and old age, clothes
folded on moth balls

and camphor, in the pad-
locked sea-chest wait-

ing for voices of children.

silence from the bed-
room where she lies

her warm flesh light
as leaves on the brass

bed where she dives
under the day's thunder:

un-
polished duncks

un-
polished screw-

on lanterns: rail-
ings through which

she looked at her
own mother's mother

smothered in cough
and carrack:

ah aaah aaaaaah
of childbirth of love

lying there with the milk
weeping through nipples

the fish face fist face
wrinkled like paper

of water, dusted with
talcum, smell-

ing of diaper green.
time drifts through the worn

sheets: the mattress
floats soddenly down

her dreams: down
the tide of grey morn-

ings when no letters
came from away where

her suns were;
when there was so

little to eat: crab
scrape stomach cramp;

when looking back
at the shadow of white

from the half-
open window, she frowned

and smiled with un-
certainty: *no*

body home?

and she hears them first
at the paling: coming

up from the beach through
the gatedoor: feet

shaking the living room
floor: crash

of joy as the china up
on the wall in the back-

room falls
from its bamboo rack.

once more she rules
from the clattering table

of sundays: ladling soup
with the curved pew-

ter ladling spoon: split
pea dumplin salt

beef squares and slices;
then rushin them off

to de tree o'clock sabbath
day school. he

gone out agen: week-
days is de co-op: more

like a fowl coop; an on fish-
fridee nights he is say

is de brederens lodge.
heavens bell cud be yell-

in far out in de sky, you
cud never budge

e from *dat* piece
o pie, an i watch-

in he pants an he ker-
chiefs; why

dese men doan know what a woman does know, nuh? all

dem lies: stale smell
o she sea-salt death

pun e breath, wrap up
like a cowl pun e skin;

de tone o' e voice re-
flexin her voice, his

eyes avoidin my eyes.

why dem starts in de night
when he breethe goin'

up up up in de dark
an de silence shape-

in' an smood
like a bowl fill-

in up wid de shak-shak
leaves an de tick-

in o crick-
ets an a cow cough-

in. but uh cahn laff
it off: uh cahn leff

e: we custom each udder
too much; too much cloze

to menn, too much pot
to scrub, too much ash

to clean out under me finger
tips, too much red

in me wailin eye; too
much cobweb to clear

from de window; too much rock
stone to brek; too much black

to push up de hill.

aaah me feet heavy
leh me pull off dese shoes

stretch de block blood out
little bit: de tiredness pass-

in like waterclouds carryin rain.

cool in hey: quiet: clock tickin but like de sun stop; de wind

an de hot season mekkin dese wooden walls
crack: de floor

boards cryin out cryin out
how de hool o' dis house like it know

me: dust drift: cock-
roach lick: moth

hole: de
tiredness passin

like waterclouds carryin

doctor?
no butter

an no more sweeten up
tea: i kin see

you int watch-
in you weight like i tell

you: tek these yellowstone pills
as it say pun de box

there: three times a day in lil
water: they will help wid de giddy

spells.
yes doctor yes doctor yes doctor yes doc

de waterclouds passin like tiredness carryin pain

but i cahn go down now
gertseen sick an want

that i look after annie
fuh she: in she baby

of eyes i kin see de shape o me own pappy
face, jess like e look in de picture.

aaah de foot bad
de tiredness passin like waterclouds carry-

an they want me to go down to half-moon tomorrow **an bring she**
    back in de rain.

so is time to get up
huh: change

into me house
cloze; put some milk

in de skillet; crack
some wolloboa wood

get de food under-
way pun de fire:

spark eye
crackle o' bone-

juice an de whole sing-
in forest on fire: whisp-

erin whips on de shiv-
erin stone o de kitch-

en where she turns
alone to the o-

ven burn-
in burn-

in world
without

world with-
out world

without
end

amen

IV

KOUMFORT

Angel/Engine

The yard around which the smoke circles
    is bounded by kitchen, latrine and the wall
    of the house where her aunt died, where

her godma brought her up, where she was jumped
    upon by her copperskin cousin
    driving canemen to work during crop

time, smelling of rum and saltfish;
    who gave her two children when, so she say,
    her back was turn to the man, when she wasn't lookin.

the children grew up quietly
    the boy runnin bout like a pump-
  kin vine, the girl name christofene

they went to st saviour primary school
    then the boy sit down an win a exam
    an gone down de hill to de college.

christie still bout here turnin foolish
    she us: ed to help me to sew
    an mek up de cloze pun de singer

sewin machine: but she fingers gone dead
    and she int got eyes in she head.
    then one two tree wutless men come up in here

an impose a pregnant pun she.
    one tek
    but de other two both foetus dead.

now she sittin up dere wid she hann in she lapp in de corner
    rockin sheself in a chair by de window
    and as far i know, she too cud be dead

2

i tek up dese days wid de zion
we does meet tuesdee nights in de carpenter shop

praaze be to god
i hear de chapman hall preacher shout out

praaaze be to god

an i hear de black wings risin
and i feel de black rock rock

praaaze be to
praaaze be to
praaaze be to gg

praaaze be to
praaaze be to
praaaze be to gg

an i holdin my hands up high in dat place
and de palms turn to

praaaze be to
praaaze be to
praaaze be to gg

an the fingers flutter an flyin away
an i cryin out

praaaze be to
praaaze be to
praaaze be to

softly

an de softness flyin away

is a black
is a bat
is a flap

o de kerosene lamp

an it spinn
an it spinn
an it spinn-

in rounn
and it stagger-
in down

to a gutter-
in shark
o' de worl'

praaaze be to
praaaze be to
praaaze be to gg

praaaze be to
praaaze be to
praaaze be to gg

de tongue curlin back
an muh face flowin' empty
all muh skin cradle an crackle an ole

i is water of wood
ants
crawlin crawlin

i is spiders weavin
away

my ball
headed head

is ancient an
black an it

fall from de top
o de *praaaze be to*

tree to de rat-
hearted coco-

nut hill.

so uh walk-
in an talk-

in: uh stepp-
in an call-

in thru
echo-

in faces
that barren an bare of my name

thru crick
crack

thru crick
crack

a creak-
in thru crev-

ices, reach-
in for i-

cicle light

who hant me
huh

who haunt me
huh

my head is a cross
is a cross-

road

who hant me
is red

who haunt me
is blue

is a man
is a moo
is a ton ton macou

is a coo
is a cow
is a cow-

itch

bub-a-dups
bub-a-dups
bub-a-dups

huh

bub-a-dups
bub-a-dups
bub-a-dups

hah

is a hearse
is a horse
is a horseman

is a trip
is a trick
is a seamless hiss

that does rattle these i: ron tracks

bub-a-dups
bub-a-dups
bub-a-dups

huh

bub-a-dups
bub-a-dups
bub-a-dups

hah

is a scissors gone *shhhaaaaa*

under de rattle an pain

i de go
huh

i de go
shhhaaaaa

an a black curl callin my name

praaaze be to
praaaze be to
praaaze be to

sh

praaaze be to
praaaze be to
praaaze be to

shang

praaaze be to
sh

praaaze be to
gg

praaaze be to
praaaze be to
praaaze be to

sssssssssssssssssssssshhhhhhhhhhh

3

an de train comin in wid de rain . . .

Peace fire

1

But my mother watches the marshalled angels
brass tinkle gong gong
the shining trumpets of the damned going forth

big bass of tuba, sousaphone and muffled drum
she observes the stiff white tune/ics, rigid blacks
the devil's shining peaks of caps and flashing instruments

the merchants got de money
but de people got de men

yes

de merchants got de money
but de people got de men

she dances a chip
step with them

hip step/chip step
one two three

and her soul goes marching on

2

i does hate black people
the sergeant-major was sayin

i hates how they grow
plundering out of the ground
snow's opposite

104

i does hate black people

they mean they stinks
they always hungry
they is mess up de white people bizness

i is watch them chase roach in de fowl yard

3

and her brothers hurled sticks stones bottles
with lighted wicks alive in them

they shattered the lights on the street
corners and stained glass in the pathways of the grey drake-
billed saracens

they raped the pale dummies: stiff foot and mannequin
in the aquarium cool of the stare window

they ripped jackets off the cellulidded widowers
they surrounded lord nelson, the island's only one-way statue

and they left him peeing through the railings of his traffic island
straight down the middle of the tourist season

they rushed into the major general's post office
declaring that the postmaster general was impotent
and that the most important postmen would be promoted generals

they entered the bank
and demanded that a bajan image dominate the currency
especially the fives the forties and the fortified

the radio stations, they announced on fm radio
would specialize in spooges, and that the national anthem
would become a hymn

written by two stooges of an ex-barbarian steel pan man
now living alone in london. from tomorrow
only buggies would be booked for private traffic in the corpor-

ate area: you may buy steal or borrow bicycles or
barrows
the institute of social and economic research

financed by ford, revived by rockefeller
would begin, until further unless otherwise notice
a four year developmental study
of harp projects and the consumption of ice

in the newer industrial parks of the island
and the connection (if any)
between drum-beat and goat-death in the sound-system hurt
of the city

4

the merchants got de monkies
an de monkies got de men

yes

de monnies got de monkies
an de monkies got de-

chip step/lann ship
one two tree

5

and we marched upon the palace
declaring that the governor was black
and that his concubines would go abroad in naturelles or afro

wigs

we entered the holy carbolic echoing church
cool clean heel heil
and the madonna was made over in the image of my sister

hale mary full of grease
the lard is with thee

rum and gourd and gumbel

6

and so with drum and cutlass, cashew stick and flugel
we ascended the steps of the steps of the steps of the house
of the man who possesses us all

and the governor was there
ace of spades in his hand
in his westcoat

and the blank manager was there
ace of clubs in his snorts
rollin golf

balls

and the virginia of our dreams
black like all the pearly people of the gates
and upon her forehead was a legend reading

BABYLON THE GREAT MOTHER OF HARLOCKS AND ABOM-
    INATIONS

deliver us

and upon her belly was a snake
her bottom plumed with psychedelic fire

Mid/Life

1

From the centre of my death
rain

drop of chad
pain of stone

drifting to green
fields

cry
tears of bone

flesh: sea
moss of hair

mud of eyes
light

2

the child
is born to splinters

broken islands
broken homes

driftwood of beaches

3

the midwife reaches black
into my tomb

and finds silence
womb

stones still
bombed babies

she hears darkness crawling up the smoothness of the cave

she hears the whistle of bats
their dracula whiskers

rank nuzzle

4

i am born/torn
with my navel string/cut

like a cracked egg
leaking

5

there is weeping on the pavements

bare feet: crocus bag shirts
shuffle

there is weeping by the window
pushed up by its stake in the canefields

6

north point from here, the lighthouse searches for salt for dead
souls

7

the windmills are swinging swinging
the cog wheels are turning turning

the crushed heart of the cane is burning burning

8

there is weeping in the front room
where christ is the guest of this house
and young princess margaret pats the patience of her horse
face smiling smiling smiling

there is weeping by the berbice chair
its long cool carved by my brother
its curved wildcane back still alive with the fingers of weavers
its crisscrosses and squares, starred silences, still holding the heat of
    my body
its wooden feet swivelled back under its arms

there is weeping by the table with the framed photo
my face muffled in black today
and its vase of paper roses

there is weeping by the walnut radio
once crackled to life by a wire clipped:
alligator teeth: to the car battery: clamped
to the arteries of sugar-loading trucks on the plantation

the car had two horns: black bubble bugle: *paa paa paadoo*
and the round electric button nose inside the steering wheel:
aa aa aaoooooga: which we all preferred

and when the radio was lit and humming: boston cinncinnati bbc:
    we heard
herr hitler goebbels winston churchill joe
louis the fourteenth half-
killing the germans and the lucky strike hit parade

9

now the old man opens his eyes to his death
and watches me squeezed through the birth of my mother's sighs

push
tug
boulder of blood
the moon's gravestones

the midwife encircles us all

her hands have known flesh
have known health
felt the black damp rip or drift
through the torn fresh

baby grandfather
new born centurion
both blind both blind
watching the shadows of water that fall from the dark of the wall
    of the spirits

10

so my youth fades slowly forward to these soft spoken grey hairs
prickles on my great grandfather's cheek

he runs behind a ball that hops and crashes
through the pains that are my eyes

i trickle from him slowly
to my son

towards my ancient children

Driftword

1

But my mother rails against the fearlures of these comforts

she stifles a dream as the whip raids her
and she calls on glint, echo of shell
the protein burning in her dead sea eyes

on those who will say no to distortions
who will pick up the broken stones
sloping them with chip and mallet out of the concave quarries

who will sharpen them to blocks, to bricks, to unwrecked boulders
who will build bells, space that the hands shape, koumforts

for her history is long and will not always bleed on other people's
    edges:
shards, shreds, broken tools, cast off political clothing, spittle of
    monkey parsing

so she dreams of michael who will bring a sword
ploughing the plimpler black into its fields of stalk,
of flowers on their stilts of future rising
who will stand by the kitchen door and permit no stranger en-
    trancement

gabriel who will mount trumpets of words:
sandbox spinnaker eyes uncracking with lightning
startling downcasts and wounds back into courage
calling her children home

and the soft spoken uriel vial to whom she will render the secrets
    of herbs

they will light wicks to honour her circle
standing all night to hinder her ghosts from rising from surface
    of mirrors
through the long wax of stars and the blood's surfage

with these suns in her house
seed she has lit
pour of her flesh into their mould of bone
the peace of the lord is upon her

lost: they will single her out
hurt: they will balm her
afraid: she will find their flicker underneath her door

they will light lip to bottle or barrel
tossing explosions into the midst of her enemies' eyes
preserving her skin from the scorpion's torch
from the touch of leprosy lies

from the dark where she plants them: blind pods
they will wait: cutting their reeds
jagged eared knives working on wood
wreathing their own words

2

so she swims through salt
dearth of blood
and her eyes close on leaves, death of love,
and she knows the wet breath of the surgeon's chloroform knife

and there is nothing to do
but become worm
again: there is no warm embrace
of calyx, kiss or the calm of translucent egg

her eyes, vivid like the pinpricks of cobblers
like the nibble of stars, open

113

their cries to the dark:
her bones stretching lazily out to the black

lake of interior mirrors.
she has become her own skin and is only her
skin: dissolving into the tonelles of roots
the muffled echoes of tar

hags she cannot remember are here
old women with teeth destroyed by time's acid
by the slow pull of hunger
the calcium suck of a hundred lispering children

aunts whose dresses are folded away
hats the family didn't destroy
roses faded to paper
and she loses her feet and her fingers

for her head is a life time away from her
belly and her hair drifts loose from its cubicles
a scissors tail figment of fish snips the smile away from her fore-
    head
as the weight of her bones lift her up and away from the tide

so she lies
mutter of echoes, folded to silence
surrounded by the multiple deaths of her children
surrendered to their ancient histories

their hopes walking like rain across the distant water

3

now she is littered with memories
an old man rakes leaves in the yard
and she turns on her side as she listens

the doctor will not be coming today

his stethoscope is screamless
it has become a pipe of peace
his black bag carries balloons
santa claus is his nomen

up the slope of the beach a crab pauses
flickering white beads of ground stone spotted with coral
in a day lazy with sea-wrack and glisten, the richness
of the day's candle wind burning with iron and blue

the crab pauses

raising its flat seeds of eyes
listening down to the thunder coming up from the curve of the
    bay
then sideways to scuttles, making necklace of dots on the day

and a wave follows, sweeping

4

as she touches again the salt and wet of his kisses

she is his secret limestone cavern
mothered from hiss and cobalt
and his breath is leaves

her own lips tingle with sea-grape
the yellow curl of cashew
and the leathery red of the fat-pork that burn on the cattlewash
    dunes

she has become the pools of his island: conch lobster flying fish
    scales

closing her eyes, he can hear the breakers breaking in her bleak
    of bone

blue surge, white leap of blood, soft crackle of pebble
and the small dead cells of the sea shells crying under that watery
  rule

holding her now, she is the bright beast of bathsheba:
dark rock unceasingly martyr'd:
nemwrack of reef's lamentations arising out of the distantest
  pool

5

now she lies forgetting the taste of the mullet
yellow roe of the sea-egg melting its metal
away from the tang of her spittle

aie yae yae
cry the forked trees
widened by sudden lightning

aie yae yae
cries the bull in the child's eyes of kites
angels alive in her heaven

echo of river trickle worn stone
until rolling downwards from softness to driftward
she knows that her death has been born

6

if it be so

let it be clay that the potter uses
and he will curve her hollow cheek and carve her darkness

if it be so

let it be stone that the sculptor smashes
and there will be her breasts, rising in sea light

116

let it be straw and weave and raffia
grass and vine and spanish needle

and there will be the cane rows of her hair

let it be hand and clap and tambour
and she will praise the lord

so that losing her now
you will slowly restore her silent gutters of word-fall

slipping over her footsteps like grass
slippering out of her wrinkles like rain

re-echo of the stream and bubble
re-echo of the cliff and scarface mountain

past the ruinate mill and the plantation stable
past the bell and the churchwall, the chapel

half-trampled with cordia leaves: the graveyards of slaves

past the scramble of grape where the train line once ran
past the boulders and stumps of the silkcotton trees

linking linking the ridges: the matchbox wood houses
past the glimmering downward of gully and pebble and fountain

the ancient watercourses

trickling slowly into the coral
travelling inwards under the limestone

widening outwards into the sunlight
towards the breaking of her flesh with foam

Notes

p. 3, 1. 4. *st philip:* the largest most southerly parish of Barbados, where the poem begins. Here is wide, bleak, wind-beaten plain, moving in terraces up the twelve steps of the island to the 'Scotland' district in the north-east (Bathsheba, Cattlewash, Chalky Mount) where the poem ends. Because of the porous limestone, and because the water flowing down the ridges does not have more than ten miles to travel, the island, though garden-canefield green in most places, has no distinctive river and very few lakes.

p. 3, ll. 7, 8. *the harbour river* and *josé, the water of the portuguese:* the harbour river (actually called the Constitution River) flows into the harbour of Bridgetown though it has become so sluggish (obstruction, pollution) that the city fathers filled it in near the city centre to make a new bus stand and market. Jose (José's) river flows east from the high lands and reaches the sea at Bathsheba-Cattlewash; but is so small and noiseless, it is seldom seen by to-day's motoring Barbadians.

The Portuguese were the first European discoverers of the island, settled by the English in 1627.

p. 3, 1. 14. *carved footsteps:* long before the European, the Amerindian Arawaks lived here and we still stumble upon their artifacts. Indeed it is my instinct that certain features of our eastern landscape (Cove, Pico Teneriffe, Indian Ground) were ceremonial monuments for our ancestors.

p. 6, 1. 9. *de excursion train out to t'ickets:* a simple railway system connecting the main sugar areas with the port and city was established in 1881 and remained in service, with several stops and starts, until 1937 when it was replaced by road and lorry transport. But while it lasted, the train was a tremendous phenomenon in our lives; so much so that even today the gods Shango and Ogoun often manifest themselves as locomotives (see 'Angel/Engine', pp. 97–103. T'ickets (thickets) was a stop on the journey.

p. 7, 11. 16, 17. *poor backra:* (buckra) is Afro-Caribbean (from a similar Ibo word) for white man/boss man. 'Poor backra', however, refers to the 'red legs', descendants of 17th-century indentured servants who persist as a kind of white maroon group to this day.

p. 8. *SAM LORD:* one of our historical/mythological figures; a kind of English pirate who from his 'castle' (now an hotel for tourists) used,

119

by placing lanterns in his coconut trees, to light ships on to the reefs that run along the whole Atlantic coast of the island.

p. 8, l. 6. *lakes, green pond, constitution river, glitter bay:* our visible waters. Lakes and Green Pond are (again) in the Scotland district; Glitter Bay, on the west coast (now nearly all sold out to tourists) is one of the most beautiful bathing beaches in the world.

p. 8, l. 13. *ragged point:* the place where St Philip turns towards the full Atlantic coast of the Arawaks; our nearest point to Africa and the rising sun.

p. 8, l. 14. *oistin town:* fishing village on the sunset side of the island.

p. 8, l. 17. *candle; book; bell:* universal ikons; but in our people's churches (as distinct from those of the establishment) the candles change from white to red to green to black, according to the occasion; the book is made of bread or cake ('book of confectionery'); and the bell is used as censer, like a calabash or vial of libation, as a summons to the spirits, as a defiance (with a sound like breaking glass) against the evil eye. Above all, it is used to express the *emotion* of the celebrant.

p. 8, l. 18. *vèvè:* signs or habitations made on the floor of chapel, 'bood', or hounfort to welcome gods, spirits, loa, powers, ancestors.

p. 12, l. 15. *mauby:* a popular Bajan (and Guyanese) frothy-headed and bitter-sweet drink, often made from the prepared bark of lignumvitae. *kukoo:* similar to the West African fufu and made and prepared in much the same way from corn(meal), yam, or breadfruit.

p. 17, l. 9. *djukas:* one of the groups of so-called 'Bush Negroes' of Surinam, who created (and retain) an impressive Afro-maroon culture in the swamplands of the Guianas during the period of slavery; as did the 'maroons of scar and cockpit country' in Jamaica.

p. 17, l. 10. *boscoes:* the word occurs in English as *bosk* meaning dark thicket, dark wood; and in Yoruba and other West African languages with the same meaning. In Barbados, *boscobelle* (p. 50) was one of our few truly maroon areas.

p. 20, l. 8. *the virgin of guadeloupe:* a rare black sacred figurine (most of the Church's Virgins are white) once taken on a traumatic tour of some of the Catholic communities of the Caribbean.

p. 39, l. 29. *meroë:* ancient centre of African culture.

p. 43, l. 4. *conkey; pone:* a kind of cake or pudding, but neither (West African *kenke*), made from pumkin, coconut or cassava.

p. 47, 11. *a grave:* slaves often buried their dead within their cabin.

p. 48. Section 4 is an anti-praise (or curse) poem, found in African tradition.

p. 48, l. 17. *monkey:* name given to the clay pitchers made by the potters of Chalky Mount (see 'Woo/Dove', p. 41).

p. 48, l. 23. *the plague dog:* the plague was the cholera of 1854 which swept the Caribbean, killing 20,000 in Barbados alone. The dog appears again in 'Cherries', p. 80.

p. 62, l. 8. *nam:* secret name, soul-source, connected with *nyam* (eat), *yam* (root food), *nyame* (name of god). *Nam* is the heart of our *nation-language* which comes into conflict with the cultural imperial authority of Prospero (O'Grady), pp. 58–64.

p. 62, l. 9. *ku late:* an example of the white man/slave master trying to use nation-language for 'look, it's too late now'.

p. 63, l. 8. *stick likkin an warrikin trix:* two references to the martial art of stick fighting particularly popular, in Barbados, among the peasants of the 'Scotland' district. *Warrick* is actually the name of the game in certain parts of Jamaica.

p. 63, l. 16. *plimpler:* thorn.

p. 64, l, 9. *nomminit:* nation-language sound/word for 'cultural domination', literally 'the gobbling up of the (other's) name'.

p. 65. *TUK* (or bumbatuk): Bajan survival of West African masquerade.

pp. 67–76. *DAIS* and *NIGHTS.* This sequence is based upon an incident that took place at Port Royal, Jamaica, during the 1820s and is to be found in the *British Parliamentary Papers on Slavery and the Slave Trade*, though it is also part of our collective unconscious and I cannot now say whether I wrote the poem before or after reading the passage. Mistress Jackson was the wife of a missionary, and the *Papers* record Ann's account in part: 'Another time I had a puppy in mistress's room feeding; Miss Elizabeth Jackson came out of bed, and wanted the puppy; I did not give it to her, and said I was feeding it; when Miss Elizabeth said I told a lie, I was not feeding the puppy. Mistress turned around, and told me to put the puppy in my lap, which I did in a passion. Mistress said I must feed the pup, when I said its belly was full; Mistress then jumped out of bed, and flogged me with a supple-jack till it broke in two, when she boxed and thumped me.'

p. 67, l. 9. *clickin' up sticks:* a game, similar to 'pick-ups', which girls play with pebbles or small stones. The narrator's meaning becomes clearer, however, when we know that *de folly* (same line) is a red-light district in an underprivileged section of Bridgetown.

p. 74, ll. 23–25. *nan:* negation of *ann* and corruption of *nam*, used here to indicate the sound of the supple-jack, taking us back to the auction block.

121

p. 77, 1. 5. *black kites flying on what should be a holiday:* in many parts of the world, kite-flying takes place as a celebration of spring (the winds of April/Easter) and the sky is alive with buzzing, sighing colour. But here the image of black kites is used to represent a kind of total public mourning.

p. 80, 1. 4. *kukoo; okro; jug:* Afro-Bajan dishes (see also pp. 12 and 38) with secret ancestral connotations.

p. 84, 1. 17. *luo:* Nilotic people who migrated into lacustrine East Africa in the period 1500–1900 and now live mainly on the eastern shores of Lake Victoria.

p. 97, ff. The god of lightning, Shango, frequently combined with Ogoun, god of iron, often manifests himself in the Caribbean as a locomotive engine; sometimes, as here, as both horse and engine.

p. 101, 1. 14. *ton ton macou* (or *macoute*): bogey figure, in this case from Haitian folk culture; literally uncle or old man (*ton ton*) with satchel or bag (*macoute*), usually used to frighten children.

p. 105, 1. 14. *lord nelson:* Barbados was the second of Britain's colonies to erect a statue to the naval hero soon after his fatal victory. Predictably, the Bajan statue stands in Trafalgar Square.

p. 117, 1. 3. *cane rows* (or *corn rows*): African manner of styling hair.